Over Land, Over Sea

Poems for those seeking refuge

edited by Kathleen Bell, Emma Lee and Siobhan Logan

introduced by Sir Martyn Poliakoff

Give me your tired, your poor,
Your huddled masses yearning to breathe free,
The wretched refuse of your teeming shore.
Send these, the homeless, tempest-tossed to me,
I lift my lamp beside the golden door!

Emma Lazarus, 1883

... everything that can be done will be done to make sure our borders are secure and make sure that British holidaymakers are able to go on their holidays.

David Cameron, 2015

Over Land, Over Sea

Poems for those seeking refuge

edited by Kathleen Bell, Emma Lee and Siobhan Logan

introduced by Sir Martyn Poliakoff

Five Leaves Publications
www.fiveleaves.co.uk

Over Land, Over Sea

Poems for those seeking refuge

edited by Kathleen Bell, Emma Lee and Siobhan Logan

Published in 2015 by
Five Leaves Publications,
14a Long Row, Nottingham NG1 2DH
www.fiveleaves.co.uk
www.fiveleavesbookshop.co.uk

ISBN: 978 1 910170 28 1

All proceeds from this volume will be donated to:
Médecins Sans Frontières
Leicester City of Sanctuary
Nottingham and Nottinghamshire Refugee Forum

Cover design, layout and typesetting by Pippa Hennessy

Printed in Great Britain

Contents

Introduction

"The days were cheerful in spite of the sound of shells bursting and machine gun fire but the nights were terrifying. We slept in the dining room. The front door bell used to ring more than once during the night and we would be accused by one side or the other of showing a light, which we were not, and threatened with dire consequences if we continued. From time to time people would rush in, having picked up gossip. Generally their news was that the Bolsheviks were about to arrive and we were all to have our throats cut. The only person on whom this seemed to make any impression was my grandmother who would get out of bed repeating, 'What will be, will be.'"

These words were written by my father, Alexander Poliakoff, describing how he remembered the start of the Russian Revolution in Moscow when he was just seven years old. A few years later, the family were refugees. Happily they were accepted by Britain and made new lives here. Their children and grandchildren have grown up and thrived here in the UK.

In my own case, most of my adult life has been spent living in Beeston and being part of the community. So it is hard to ignore the plight of families who are going through traumas today similar to those experienced by my father and grandparents nearly a hundred years ago.

This book is a really impressive collection of poetry and prose put together by a group of East Midlanders who care passionately about the lives of others and who are determined to help those less fortunate than themselves. Everyone who has contributed has done so free of charge and all of the proceeds from the sales are intended to help refugees.

It is a great demonstration of the spirit which exists in our region. It also shows that compassion is still alive in the UK and that we are willing to welcome new families into our country so that they too can contribute to our communities as soon as they have overcome their dreadful experiences. Until then, we need to help them.

Sir Martyn Poliakoff CBE FRS,
Beeston, Notts, November 2015

The Man Who Ran Through the Tunnel

When I heard
how he ran
across continents
over rivers
through forests
through deserts
and through tunnels,
how could I fail
to be inspired?

Ambrose Musiyiwa

Frontiers

for Teddy Buri, NLD

The Elsinore strawberries hung in their syrup
like air balloons in a red sky.
Seville orange slivers, marinated overnight

in Jameson Whisky, lay cross-hatched
in gelatinous amber.
Carefully wrapped for the flight,

they nestled in my rucksack,
refugees from my overweight case.
But they were not allowed—

they might be explosive,
the percentage of liquid to solid too high.
I pleaded their case—presents for my host,

home-made. *That's worse*, they said.
Would you like them? I asked the young woman
who tried to be kind.

Not allowed.
I'd like to think, at the end of the day,
when no one was looking,

she reached in the bin of disposed of possessions
and rescued my jars.
I hadn't lost my clothes, I hadn't lost

my childhood in photographs,
I hadn't lost my country.
And still it cut me to the quick.

As the plane lifted from my country
I thought of you fleeing to the border
with your life, only knowing

you were near to the camp
when you woke in the jungle
to the barking of dogs.

Chrissie Gittins

What We Know

This is what I know:
we walked across Ghor to Farah and then
through Turkmenistan round the Black Sea, the Caspian,
into a wall marked 'Europe'.
We cheated the borders of Hungary. I know
friends in the camp who choked in lorries
across a thousand miles, into Italy without
a word. I know that this camp
is on flatland above the sea;
full of gulls and tourists who can choose
to ignore the heavy-steeled temptation
of a dark tunnel and its trains.
I know that call.

This is what you do not know:
the soft valleys of the Ghor. High mountains
round the hometown of Chaghcharan.
Carpet-weavers who cannot read a word
but surely make thread sing. A woman
taking the place of a man; driving a car.
You do not know our radio; The Voice of Peace.
Here is my son, Aymal, who must keep
bloody secrets. And my wife. You do not know
how a man outside the camp at Sangatte
knocked my phone to the floor as it rang. My wife.
You do not know these people.

Kerry Featherstone

What's in a name?

Reem is so tired his legs quiver like a fawn's.
Elias prays to God. He asks 'Why?'
Firas understands. He has to be brave.
Uri cries in the dark, praying for dawn.
Ghaith's tears fall in time with the rain.
Ephrem passes an apple to his sister, his stomach growls.
Elham smiles, takes a bite and passes it back.

Penny Jones

Channel Crossing

Above decks the blue sky cries seagulls
and a dragged pull of cirrus cloud.
Children against the railings
hauled back by parents:
'Can we go for chips, mum?'
The ferry heaving under,
bulging a cargo of fruit machines, TV lounges
and cheap French wine.

Below decks it is quiet with the stink of petrol.
Stephan shifts
feels the push of Jolanta's foot against his thigh.

Fourth run today.
The captain, thinking about home, wonders what's for tea
and will he be back in time for the match?
They could do with a washout, his team,
that or a miracle.
They never should have sold their striker to United.

The lorry is hot, sealed against curious eyes,
lettering on the side advertising a supermarket chain.
The swell of the sea
shifting bodies against each other in the cramped space.

A prayer comes to Stephan
a meditation.
He speaks it silently to himself,
        careful of the precious supply of air.
He thinks of the dress he will buy Jolanta
of the children they will have.

'I feel sick, mum.'
'Go to the toilet, then. I told you not to have them chips.'
The ferry heaving
the sky blue above
the hold airless, petrol-laden, bumper to bumper full.

After,
when Stephan comes to me at the refugee centre,
the only thing he can remember about the boat
is the moment that Jolanta's foot
stopped moving against his thigh.

Anne de Gruchy

Backscatter Song

Scanning now. Please wait...
There's something organic
hidden in this freight.
I see blood and panic.

There's something organic
showing up bright white.
I see blood and panic
captured in my light.

Showing up bright white,
clear as contraband
captured in my light:
aliens. May not land.

Clear as contraband,
I see desperation.
Aliens may not land
without documentation.

I see desperation
hidden in this freight
without documentation.
Scanning now. Please wait...

Joanne Limburg

The word *backscatter* refers to a kind of x-ray technology which can be used to obtain particularly bright and detailed images of materials—such as explosives, firearms, drugs and human beings—which might otherwise remain undetected.

Consignment

Somehow his scent
had slipped the end of shift sniffer dogs
the lazy wave of a heartbeat wand.

Slotted like a rock climber's
abandoned cam between steel cases.
When did his footprints

last leave their signature in the sand?
He's cold, cold as desert night, but met
by the warmth of a soft voice.

He hears only the softness,
tastes sandwiches that respect his faith.
As his erstwhile liberator recognises

himself, all men and women
in the black mirror of those wide eyes,
before they arrive to take him away.

Martin Johns

Accusations

There is so much talk
of swarms in the tunnels,
hordes on the boats,
masses storming the borders,
cockroaches on benefits.
And then there is that photograph
of one little boy washed up on a beach,
his feet pointed towards the shore,
his face buried in the sea,
his small body that could be my son or yours,
that says we should be ashamed of ourselves.

Aoife Mannix

A Consolation

The dead do not come back to us,
they harbour in the recesses,
lodging in abandoned spaces;
between the said and the undone.

We can but weep awkwardly,
knowing our end is not far
from an encroaching shoreline
and a drawn out ancient ritual.

Our sorry consolation—
a translated hail and farewell.

Mahendra Solanki

We Walk Together

Our family waits for news.
We know of dangers
but have no weapons.

We have legs and
we stand up;
we will walk together.

It is hot
but they share water and plums from their garden.
Tarek's false leg gives him pain but Tomas offers a ride
on his bicycle.

Amira's feet are bleeding, Sayid gives her his trainers.
The children laugh as he dances a *dabka* in his wife's
silk slippers.
We all smile.

We walk when they walk,
sleep when they sleep,
light rain beading our blanket.

Under the same sun,
the same moon,
our family waits for news.

Sally Jack

Callum's Day

It's Callum's Day. Along the avenue
there is a procession in his honour.
Rank upon rank of motherly women,
each with a basket of fresh-picked flowers.
Schoolchildren, clutching Callum's teddy bears.
Senior police officers, with medals.
Civic dignitaries, in chains of office.
Representatives from local churches.
Media. The medical profession.
Folk from caring organisations.
Everyone has turned out for Callum's Day
except, sadly, his closest relatives,
whom the authorities were unable
to contact, although they tried very hard.
And Callum himself, appropriately,
on Callum's Day, is in his rightful place,
at the forefront of the whole assembly,
carried by a single undertaker.
Callum, who brought nothing into this world,
takes nothing from it, true to tradition,
except 'Callum', a label printed to him
for use on the occasion of Callum's Day.
Callum the refugee, who, like many
refugees before him and many since,
managed to make it across the border,
only to be turned around and sent straight back.

Peter Wyton

In 2002 an abandoned newborn was found on the site being developed for the Commonwealth Games. He was named Callum and passed away a few hours after being found.

Life History

1
He finds his sister's glove
among the bootprints in
a snowdrift near the wood.

2
He takes it with him when
he hikes across the mountains,
begging bread from strangers.

3
A new identity
he never quite gets used to
acquaints itself with others.

4
He takes to languages
like landscapes: in each
a job, a girl, a question.

5
When he crosses the ocean
he watches herring gulls
competing for his wake.

6
The woman who becomes
his wife and bears him sons
(no daughter) brings him luck.

7
The hands he labours to
keep occupied attempt
a kind of tenderness.

8
He takes no interest
in politics, but sport
absorbs the idle hours.

9
He examines a face
in the mirror, no longer
his sister's younger brother.

10
He sings his granddaughter
a foreign song, but stops
when she bursts into tears.

11
Woken by explosions
when the century ends,
he takes a sleeping pill.

12
With nothing left of what
he once imagined all
there was, he wants for nothing.

Gregory Woods

Come In

For the migrants and refugees arriving in Europe

We are sorry for our neighbours,
those of them that do not know
the way to show a welcome;
they have read the book of doors
but forgotten how they open.

We are sorry for the landlord,
he's always been a problem
and the agents in his office,
need we say they do not act—

to be more clear:
they do their nothing
not on our behalf.

Sorry for the state in which you find us,
it isn't like we didn't know you would be coming
and for the pains we know you've suffered;

please be easy, slip your shoes off,
take this blanket
it's the least that we can do.

I am sorry for our manners,
when we visited you last
the mess we left,
the reason you have had to call today.

Lydia Towsey

For Aylan

I just wanted you to know
your lovely bones have not been wasted
that your tiny little body in a picture on a beach
made the world sit up and notice that you're there

and I know it's much too late
and you'll never be a father or a lover or a man
but your passing in the tide has helped the families
who follow in your wake

and this will never make your mother feel better,
feel at peace, but I wanted you to know
that your tiny little body in a picture on a beach
forced the powers of the world to rally round

and babies shouldn't die in plastic dinghies in the night
while their parents flee the trouble that we caused
and the people selling arms to the Middle Eastern maniacs
should not be leading countries
telling lies
making wars

and I just wanted you to know
your lovely bones have not been wasted
that your tiny little body in a picture on a beach
made the world sit up and notice that you're there
take care
sleep tight
little one

Laura Taylor

Citizens

If you smile when you're stopped and empty your pockets
For the officer who stopped you last night
        You're one of us.

If your sister dances with whoever she likes
Whenever she wants and you don't sit late
In the kitchen, waiting
        You're one of us.

If some of your best friends are white
But you won't bring them back to the folks,
If you know the metres of cloth it takes
To wrap a sari, the number of suras in the Qu'ran
        You're one of us.

If you're sure we'll score the winning goal
In a penalty shoot out semi-final,
If you can recite three Shakespeare sonnets,
Two soliliquies and the ending to Cymbeline,
        You're one of us.

If when you hear someone say on
The bus, 'I'm not racist but...'
You turn and refuse to accept that caveat,
        You're one of us.

Ken Evans

Alright, Jack?

No, Jack.
I'm not alright.
Not by a long shot.
When did it become
the British thing to do
to coldly turn our backs
on people in desperate situations?
When did it become
the British thing to do
to talk about and treat people
as if they are the scum of the Earth?
When did it become
the British thing to do
to just shrug our shoulders
and ignore the suffering
of fellow human beings?
When did it become
the British thing to do
to be so full of hate?
No, Jack.
I'm not alright.
Not by a long shot.

Alan Mitchell

The Whiteness

The first white lab mouse to be sent to the moon
Died in the rocket, a pocket-sized
Martyr to the cause of discovery.

The next two
Survived.

Alas, alas, were never retrieved.
How the moon received them was anyone's guess.
Was she cold to her littlefooted guests in their furs?
Was she even habitable?

I'd like to think they made a life there.
Multiplied and thrived and evolved to survive
Sans water, sans air, somehow
In their unfamiliar expansive lair.

Meanwhile their families back at the lab
Muse on their lost ones and hope and pray
That wherever they went took pity on them
And take pity on us, amen, amen.

Meanwhile, in his labcoat, of a night he'll stare
At the moon and under her diffused soft glare
Will squint and think he saw the surface move
He swore he saw the surface move.
And the movement moves and moves and moves

Mariya Pervez

Birthdays, May 2015

We were celebrating birthdays.
Out to lunch with our son.
His birthday was coming up.
Elsewhere babies were being born.
St Mary's hospital—a straightforward birth
but it made all the newspapers.
Guns fire in Hyde Park.
Another birth lost in the statistics
on a sinking boat
between Libya and Italy
as the mother is plucked from the sea.
Guns fire in Syria and Eritrea.
In our restaurant
how should we react?
We have heard the alarm
but see no danger.
Meanwhile
one baby goes home.
The other is one of 600 rescued,
homeless, looking for a home,
mourning those whose journey
ended in the sea.
We are assembled
outside the restaurant
before returning
to finish our lunch.
And what is more
we do not pay the bill.

Merrill Clarke

Diwan Under Snow

This night I'm the Kurdest Farzad
from my birth's give & take to my hands' no-raised hand
from the erection of two fingers, the pinkie & first of the
    fist/heist,
between all the angels of five & fifty & fifty thousand &
    fifty million
the Kurdest fourteenth night full moon

the heart is shaking
dried lips are shaking
lead of the bullet's chest is shaking
the no colour in your face is shaking
you have neither mother nor sister
nor a home to be bailed from/out into
not a friend to kick away your gallows stool
not a trigger in your pocket, ripped-out lining,
not even a shroud to be buried in, not a blood home,
no way   you even don't have an even
you don't even have your own shadow
you don't, no you don't, you do not
                have

two-windowed worry-eyes
warmness of little-fires & chandeliers behind all
    windows, know
such that you're worried about the balcony,
the diwan that went sleeping beneath the snows &
    became crazy
the table that sat down under the snow so as not to
    appear bare

the woman who white-combed her hair under the snows
poetry poured so pure that the snow lost its white
the loneliness of black-cracked finger-nails
open wounds under ripped-open shirts
the sole witness to the limping revolver-bouts
that run around after an imam's horse
& end up under some bung-cart of green groceries

Death would drown in its own shy sweats
this death if it had feet would flee
if it was human & had a head would bang its head on a tree
or like a stranger-poet from its forearm would fashion a
        balalaika
and strum it naked under the snow
balalaika   balalaika   bailalaila lailai
    lailalai la   lai lie sleep now
  my bairn

Ziba Karbassi (translated by the poet with Stephen Watts)

in a shroud of semantics

if you keep speaking
as though I had a choice
when I'm running
from what you created
then nothing can touch you
in your inaction
none can bring you
to accept your blooded hands
in this shameful reality

if you keep abandoning me
on those desolate beaches
limbs akimbo face down
head pointed towards home
then only you can cry
your crocodile tears
for your constituents' sake
much too late too late
now the damage is done

if you keep shunting me
around these heartless sidings
to leave me going nowhere
frustrated and fearful
then you will come
to find yourself immured
by the very hypocrisies
that strip you of integrity
and make mud of your name

John Mingay

Relativity

You think there's a gap between us
You think we are separate   distinct
You think Newton had it right   that we collide
and come apart   collide
and come apart   But
this is Einstein's world   A hundred
years ago   he showed how
we all are bound   I nudge space
and you
are shifted
You think if you're high enough
you're safe   You think
when I fall   your orbit
is unaltered   You think
this poem
is just physics
Think again

Tania Hershman

from **The Riverside Commission**

i.
the A frame stretched tight
against a familiar sky

take a step, a start

ii.
a canal, a river
through a lost green corridor
a well-kept secret

iii.
a man runs on this path
between grass and water
like a feverish race horse
blinkered against distractions

iv.
a to and fro
a giant sea-saw rocking

a give and take:
the hiss and spill of the past

v.

we who left behind our lands
we who crossed the black ocean
we who miss the open fields and running water

we seek comfort in this pull of green
we seek rest in this flowing bed

Mahendra Solanki

Blue Folder

"What's your favourite colour?" I said.
"Blue," you said.
We'll get you a blue folder then... a blue folder to put all
    this in.
He had been walking around with his paperwork in a
    plastic bag.
A plastic bag the photographers gave him when they took his
    photo for the UKBA.

A plastic bag for the letters from his counsellor,
His doctor, his caseworker, his social worker, Foundation
    for the Victims of Torture.
It's not nice to walk around with papers like this in a
    plastic bag, I said.
We'll buy you a folder, a blue folder, make it all better.

You didn't talk much on the way there, I sat quietly with you;
    in your silence.
Your silent place that is haunted with your screaming,
    as they tortured you.
With the screaming you can hear of others, as they were
    being tortured.
With your mother crying, with the distance you ran with
    them shooting bullets after you.
With the pain of wanting your mother, and your brother,
    and your family.
In that silent place I sat with you, although I am not privy
    to the screaming.
A silent place filled with loud pain.

I can see your unshaven face.
I can see where your hood hides you so nobody can see you.
I can see you hide behind a tree, or look nervously away
when you think you are overheard.
I can hear the trembling in your voice, and how sometimes
you speak in a barely audible tone.
I can hear all that, but I cannot hear the screams inside
your head.

The letter from the GP was good we said, good.
15 cigarette burns on your right arm, seven on your left.
Marks on your upper and lower body consistent with
electrocution;
With being hit with iron bars, and heavy metal objects.
A page... line after line.
Descriptions of the marks consistent with torture.
It was a good letter, yes.
We will buy you a folder to put it in, with all the others,
make it all better.

We sat on the train, the sunshine reminds you of home.
Home... a place you miss, home... a place your family are in.
Home... the place you went to university.
Home... the place you are so homesick for now.
"Is there anything you want to tell us?" said the lady at the
asylum screening interview.
"I don't want to go home," you said.

We sat in the sun and we played backgammon, that didn't
make it better.
I brought you a croissant and fizzy apple juice, that didn't
make it better.
I asked you what films you liked and you told me, and then
you told me how they took your computer.
I wanted to say we can make it better...

A blue folder, that's it, a blue folder, we'll put all this in a
blue folder.
Your favourite colour, that will make it all better.

Lily Silverman

The Insurrection of Poetry

Poems are on the march.
They are singing
from the rubble of Ground Zero,
the ruins of Damascus and Sarajevo,
the bomb shelters of Amiriyah,
the poisoned bodies in Halabja,
from the mouths of murdered men folk
in Srebrenica.

Poems are growing from their winding sheets
in the mud and trenches
of butchered nature.
Their guns fire white poppies.
Their flags are the colour of rainbow.
Their hands fold paper cranes
under the olive trees.
From the bones of mutilated generations
they grow blossoms of resurrection.

Listen
you tyrants, murderers,
fundamentalists, mutilators,
rapists, occupiers,
racists, persecutors,
autocrats, crucifiers,
fanatics, torturers, liars,
obfuscators, manipulators,
warmongers,

silencers.

Listen!

Poems all over the world
are saying
ENOUGH.

Chrys Salt

the trouble with words

a swarm of bees is not apt
perhaps a cloud that hums
because it has that floating feel
this in respect of bees too
for their intention is not to harm
one of these misunderstandings
when the wrong end of a stick
is picked up and becomes a cudgel
quickly becomes razor wire
barbed not being good enough these days
though clouds still travel overhead
make eyes drift towards them
in heads too troubled for words
would take to the sky if it was possible

James Bell

Relative

It's cold on the bike, and I've forgotten my gloves.
At work, the team are not playing ball.
But a pupil-searing glare

is glancing off the Mediterranean
where cotton-clad backs are pressed
to cotton-clad chests.

The coast is clear
and so is the horizon.

Roy Marshall

A Memorable Journey

After "The Horse Fair" by George MacKay Brown

Today you are going to write about an exciting or memorable journey. Remember to check your work for spelling, punctuation and grammar.

I went to the beach
we left our dog for the day with my aunt
I sat in a boat beside my mum, dad and little brother
Dad gave money to a man
the boat was crowded
mums dads babies and grandparents
we watched the waves

we heard wailing and crying
night was cold and windy
the smell of diesel and fish
blew all over the ship

the man wore a baseball cap
he took off with the crew
he struck a hammer in my heart
the rescue!—the whole boat
tipped over at the rescue—

I held on by my nails
men climbed out of the sea
someone shouted at me
are you dead or alive

the moon was gone
and my brother was gone
I was dead but they
picked me out of the sea
now I am in this country

Fantastic effort! Thank you so much for sharing.

Barbara Saunders

just before dawn

the silence	is heavy with
a lover's breath	just before dawn
a time of aloneness	freedom
smell virgin clay	wild tanglewood
on the horizon	bare blasted trees
suggest something	nothing

James Bell

supermoon
our world wide will
to blame

Helen Buckingham

Purges

(the Mediterranean passage)

after Seamus Heaney

My palms make a boat where a poem sways:
Dan Taggart, who drowns kittens–
it's better for them, he says
to the scared boy allowed to watch.

My arms ache with their weight
and the weight of refugees
lost in Mare Nostrum, Our Sea,
while I watch the evening news.

Waves lap in the hull of my hands,
words wash from the page, resurface.
The scared boy, drowned by life,
now shrugs at death, the poem says.

Perhaps those nameless men, who load
their leaky boats with fear, shrug too,
eyes closed tight in the haul
and hell and heave of life.

I hear the scrape of kittens' claws
and scoop one out, a glossy Tom, quick
as a poet's words, a ship's cat,
sleek, with knowing eyes. Alive.

Jan Harris

Landing on Lampedusa

Scoop by scoop
she drags her whole story
onto the beach.
She is a helmet towed by flippers,
scarred by sharks and rudders.

She does not have a tag,
the sharks saw to that—
so arrives on a cloudy night
in between civil wars;
when the landing area is quieter,
when fewer people come out to watch.

She heaves the cargo
she will never see alive,
but knows they are whiter
than the moon they have not seen.
Her cargo has been squirming
since the sea stopped rocking them
and this is the closest they will ever be.

For if they ever meet
after shells have hardened,
out on the waves
as they vie for a broken crab;
she will never know
she is starving her own flesh
—just by trying to live,
and that's all her blank eyes
in their leather hood can focus on.

She looks past the muddled tracks
of army, police and border patrol,
just scoops and drags herself past
the headlights that are scanning
this stranded seaweed mess.

None of this matters to her,
to her heaviness
when the moon is urging her on.
She just scoops and drags herself past
the lost bikinis, Peroni bottles
and single sandals
that had walked deserts to get here.

Laila Sumpton

Exodus

All Ramsgate knows their names: the Medway Queen,
the Prudential, Bluebird, Sundown, little Tamzine—
her trifling fifteen feet snatching a victory from Dunkirk.
The lights of Goodwin Sands mark their passage—

those paddle steamers, sloops and little ships that dodged
mines and tides, bombs and guns, again and again
carried the snared on decks that before the war served
ham and eggs, while their wooden wheels spun.

Sail 2,000 miles, 75 years. Crossing from Tripoli to
Lampedusa, four rubber dinghies sink. Parched travellers
explain money, not drowning, is the hitch. Eight foot waves.

Conditions like slave ship Zong. Frail vessels with invisible
names ghost the deep. Beyond the Harbour Brasserie
a flag flutters on the Kent front. Empty shoes carpet the sea.

Danielle Hope

In a small boat

In a small boat
On a great sea
Looking out to the horizon...
Boat is leaky
—people speak different languages.
This is no Ark.
Over days we run out of water,
Say a prayer to our maker
And look to the future.
At last we see land,
Jump ship and swim to safety.
Look out again to the horizon
And send a prayer
Across the ocean
To our fellow travellers,
Wishing them safe passage.

Louisa Humphreys

Fabric Shiver Twine

Fabric: a woven
tissue of fibres

Woven

into roadside trees
a pattern of witnesses

stitched round hundreds
of towns' cuffs

hope's frail braids

frontiers' fabrics
flap

Shiver: a flake or
splinter of stone

Clothes

sway as wind
fills fabric

clothes

shiver as water
lulls sleeves

clothes

rip as dead
thorns pretend

to be

people's hands

Twine: encircle, embrace,
coil or wind round
or about

Ahead

a road's twine
a cold cloth of hills

behind

a war's burning fabric
a sea's stinging shawl

ahead

strange sky of silk wisps

Mark Goodwin

Pedestrians

We all know who they are,
the men on the long hard shoulder
between Junctions 5 and 6,
between entry
and almost certain removal.
Home is wherever you walk
and they stride along
by the western carriageway
letting the swing of walking
take them.
Drivers, passengers,
only a few feet from them,
stare ahead down their lanes.
There is no stopping
on their motorway.
Wait till the overhead sees,
announces its kindly truisms:
PEDESTRIANS IN ROAD,
TREES IN FOREST,
BIRDS IN SKY.

Hubert Moore

Snow fall

This evening at around five o'clock
snow blizzards into the darkness
from a sky that was orange all day.
Sheet lightning flashes as it falls faster

flakes the size of billiard balls cast white
over cars, slippery walkways, hunched
figures, umbrellas, bare trees and buses
that groan towards steamy shelters.

Such snow patterned gardens evoke
other winters, snowballing in the park
shabby sculpted men with onion noses
and floppy hats; cold houses, colder outdoors.

But how would it have been my love
if we had journeyed in crueller snow
herded into trucks or to labour
beyond borders, sour

bread frozen in the hand, starved
to the frailest naked twig.
I light a candle on my table, picture your hands—
how lucky I am to know their contours,

to watch them jostle pans on your stove.
And, under wooden beams, as you slice
potatoes and bread, a soft gas flare
warms the landscapes of our skin.

Danielle Hope

The Gate of Grief

And when the monsoons came
after so many years, we followed the herds.
The air was sweet with water.
Goats and camels grazed in the meadows
and our eyes slaked thirst with green.

Later it was the scouring hunger
of desert winds; the withered grass
and bleached bones that drove us on.
At the shore of the great water, we collected
shells and weeds from rocks.
When a sharp-eyed hunter spied land over there
we began to think
how to reach this new place, how to put
ourselves into the water.

Siobhan Logan

Gate of Grief: Bab-al-Mandab, Red Sea—the point from which our earliest human ancestors embarked to leave Africa.

Promises

The salesman didn't bring a glossy brochure to the meeting.
As the sun went down across Somalia, he painted a picture
How beautiful and easy life was going to be in England,
Your own place in Bristol, Bolton or Milton Keynes,
Catching a big red bus to work, chewing khat in the café
Where all year long the sun will be
Filtering through the leaves of the broad oak tree.
The fare quoted includes all taxes, gratuities and bribes,
Port transfers, a shared cabin and a swift pantechnicon
to Calais.
"No luggage allowance." "No luggage allowed." He spoke
quickly.
Terms and Conditions apply: 75% cash now,
The rest taken on loan, relatives guaranteeing.
3 Months 0% credit, then the Invariable Rate applies.
Easily settled from wages remitted home by wire.
Off Lampedusa the boat sank. All were drowned.
The Invariable Rate now applies.
Necessary steps are being taken to recover.

Richard Devereux

Notice of Asteroid

They're coming over here, and taking our space
say the stars, the planets
the moons and supernovas.
It's not the white dwarves' burden
lament the piercing giants who,
alight for centurion light years, have known
the darkness that we, aboard this pale blue blot,
have had to offer the universe.
Mars is full. Space is full. Stop leering at our black holes,
go back to whence you came—
back to your walls, your wars, your monetised theory
    of existence.
Don't come over here, but explore yourselves first.
Or else,
You're liable for extinction.
Non-compliance will result
in Notice of Asteroid.
Celestial disregards,
Heavens Office
'for a safe, just and tolerant space'

George Symonds

Asking Directions

Be not forgetful to entertain strangers: for thereby some have entertained angels unawares. Hebrews 13.2

Where is the kingly palace,
good man, please to say?
We come to see the little king
who was born today.

"There is no kingly palace,
sirs: there is no king.
We are a poor village
and dream of no such thing."

Where are the rich men's houses
in their tended grounds?
We come to see the little lord:
there will he be found.

"There are no rich men's houses,
sirs, in all this town.
In some poor man's lodging
your lord, he must lie down."

Where then should God's son be found,
in what house or hall?
"Sirs, here is no place fitting
for God's son at all,

but if you step behind me
into the stable, sirs,
you may see Mary my wife
with His son and hers."

Sheenagh Pugh

Ave Maria

So I pushed, like an eager pilgrim, up to the shrine,
up switchbacks of calcareous rock, alternately baked
and shaded by the olives and carobs, that rock.
Then cobbles spread near the summit—a rust-lidded well
hiding in a corner—and where they flattened out
it waited with its dark door, flat white walls,
a wave of brown-tiled roof, a cracked rose window.
Bells clanked brightly down in the shadowed town
where cars pressed to and fro, on the verge of silence.
A butterfly bounced across. A plane hit a mountain
but slid out the other side like a threaded needle.
Forcing the handle made the shrine door screech

and the bus-stop-sized room seemed too dark. But there
they were,
ready to give their blessings for my offerings:
their unfitted crowns, dull and preposterous,
toppling permanently left and right;
the slit-gapped fingers of the infant reaching
like a lost conductor, fashioned with all the care
grim duty, if not talent, could bestow
seven hundred quiet years ago;
their eyes plump, lips quarter-smiling—even the child
knowing more than you, including you;
and a space in the Perspex screen to slip my hand through
and sense love bursting fresh from a cold beige foot.

Rory Waterman

Umbilical

It was a dark green Ford of '68
whatever model of cars were then
that pulled away in the green of night
beyond the garden wall.

My brother and I
watching from the porch
our mother recede.

How the lines of it were like waves,
how the cave of it retreated,
how my vision stepped behind
and I folded like a packet, gone.

So much of it across the sea
for so long. Four and five.
What boats are these.

Russell Christie

journeying

we threw
things that were heavy
overboard

they sank
we stayed afloat
we lived

they turned
into creatures of the sea
and stayed below the surface

when we reached dry land
they turned
into creatures of shadow

and followed us everywhere

Ambrose Musiyiwa

I Am Collecting Seas

I am collecting seas,
we all collect them
we all stare at them with longing.

We reach for them like reaching for the rain.
Plath wrote, they said,
there are too many poems about rain.

There are too many poems about the sea.

I am collecting seas,
some of them are old water.

There are the waves that began with
Seas are homesickness for homes we never had
and then the piano agrees.

Childhood songs of the sea
written for lost adults
lamenting the shells
like us sad humans.
We cry. We luxuriate in this.

I am collecting seas,
there's the silver baptismal water
of this bleached Australian book
winking at me in familiarity and unfamiliarity.
There's the blue that is too blue
and so, unnameable.

We write ten thousand words
on how we cannot write about it.

I am collecting seas,
the alien ones with the orange thighs
parted to the sand with colours
glistening like the backs of lizards to the sun.
Yellow upon yellow,
flesh not quite meeting the liquid.

I am collecting words,
there are too many words about the seas.

Hila Shachar

Goodbye to Theresienstadt

So Fortune has made arrangements to eject us.
It knocks on the front door with an official hand.
This isn't the first time. Once again we're being moved on
towards fresh woods. New pastures. Unfamiliar land.

Fate got us evicted from our previous homes.
It booted us about, pummelled us with its fists.
Almost we'd begun to feel that life in the camp was safe.
Now the way ahead's unclear. Our road is full of twists

and turns. Nobody knows what's going on outside;
where our families are, if loved ones have been spared.
We have become weak. The very thought of being told
our future makes us tremble. We are that scared.

Rose Scooler (translated by Sibyl Ruth)

The Election Candidates Promise to be Tough on the Causes of Disorder

Car doors secured, fathers leave for their orderly office,
Mothers leave for school with their disorderly children

Sparrows seek asylum in the orderly sunlight,
Squabble for scraps in the disorderly breeze.

At the airport, a man is detained on suspicion of
        future disorder
By officers who assure him that Britain is an orderly place

Although the man is afraid of uniforms & order
& policemen & soldiers drunk & disorderly

& is afraid of the locked room where he'll await a court order
Which may send him back to his country's civil disorder

In a van down a road that smacks of order,
Cars bound for the office, mothers & disorderly children.

Alan Baker

This

This is the tyranny, this is the fear.
This is the misery for those who live here.
This is the hatred, this is the war.
Nothing is sacred, not any more.
This is the anger, this is the pain.
This is the hunger, but this is no game.
This is the pestilence, this the disease.
There can be no resistance from down on your knees.
This is the rotten, and these are the starving.
The people forgotten when it comes to the carving.
These are the children fighting for rice.
This is globalisation, and this is the price.
This is humanity at its very worst.
This is insanity, and these are the cursed.
This is the murder and this is the rape.
This is the fervour they try to escape.
This is the boat and this is the lorry.
'This is our quota, we're terribly sorry.'
This is your great ploy to protect your own land.
This is the small boy washed up on the sand.
These are the bodies left to decay.
Whoever your God is, he's just run away.
This is your power and this is your glory.
This is the hour, the end of the story.

Mark Rawlins

Again Tonight

Crete, late summer. We take a pedalo to gather rock salt offshore. Sixteen in all, onboard and swimming alongside. We start taking in water, sitting low in the waves. Kids jump off, to let up the weight. A child cries, parents kick hard to get us to shore. We don't speak. My son clings like a monkey, my daughter studies my face. How can I hold them out of the water as well as the boy whose mum stayed behind? We get home. We have homes. Nobody drowns. But I feel sick.

And again tonight.

Anne Holloway

Outside the photograph

Sea otters don't wear pink, but she looks like one
from a wide angle, drifting with the tide.
The woman's anorak and scarves buoy her.
Zoom in and see her baby, swaddled
in a salmon-coloured sling arranged
so she lies on her mother's heartbeat, exhausted.
Her mother looks beyond the borders
of the photograph, towards the coastguard's boat.
These two will be rescued.
Clammy as wet clothes, memories will cling.
The mother's journey will pass into family lore.
The girl will later be puzzled as to why
she can only get to sleep
when she's lulled by lapping water
and the feel of another's heart.

Emma Lee

Waiting

When morning came, she knew that the people outside were not ghosts. Cautious, she stood, walked to the window, and looked. There were more than she thought. Their silence had deceived her. They were careful too. Grown-up hands steered infants away from her flower-beds. Next year's vegetable harvest was safe. A man looked up and the bundle close to his chest stirred. How unwise to bring a baby here. The man's glance caught hers, and beneath his patience she perceived a dreadful urgency. They were not ghosts—not yet. She drew the curtain across, returned to her chair, and waited.

Kathleen Bell

So Many Set Out

One was miscarried
and two born too soon,
three hatched at dawn but were eaten by noon.

Four were deprived
and five disaffected,
six were mistaken but never corrected.

Seven were stranded
and eight more were drowned,
nine were stamped 'bogus' and sent to the pound.

Ten lacked direction,
eleven finesse,
twelve met the judges but failed to impress.

Twenty were shelved
and thirty rejected,
fifty lost face and were soon deselected.

A hundred were stories
with no proper ending,
thousands undone, and a million pending.

Joanne Limburg

Ebb

And the sea shall give up
the last of its dead

before the media gives up
its corruption of words:

immigrant for *refugee*,
crisis for *tragedy*.

Neil Fulwood

Ditch

I should
focus. Middle lane crawlers,
no chance to break. Slam
on the anchors; fuck's sake.
HGVs overtaking on a hill.
Blues and twos in the mirrors,
don't spew. Thud, bang, cry,

"cash," promised the local link. Bailiff bug spray. Maybe a
cheap holiday...

"Open the window. Wake up."
Thud in the wind, the groaning road,
the chanting choir, rising decibels,
fumes; are they hearing this?
Up goes the radio. Can't ignore
the call and response. Shriek,

acid in mouth. Upcoming layby. Let them out. Stretch
their legs...

"So every fucker for miles sees?"
Shrill, back, forth. Panic blurs
front and back; animated hands,
kids cheering on a playground
fight. Chorus. Fine. Not fine.
CHECK. Serious this time.

"If they're dead, do what with cargo?"

Drag in a breath. Drive. Sometime
we have to arrive. Wind? Imagination?
Deliberations simmer, fade. Not a prayer,
knocking or plea; can't bear to say it.
They hear me though. Something's wrong.
They're shutting up. They're catching on.

Right indicate, pull over. Neutral, handbrake. Engine off.

Distance rolls from cab to back. Wrestle padlock,
rusty key, double doors, heavy. Received
by two lifeless eyes, upturned face. Squashed,
gone bad. Mass grave loose in the back.
"Check for survivors!" begs the local link.
Lock eyes, throat torn, gas station sandwich,

not a rattle of breath. Women and children encased in
dead men.

"You dumpster dive. Fuck this."
The link lingers, hops foot to foot;
legs, gelatin, reach him, grab
his shirt, haul him after the others.
Twitch, double think. Go along, just

ditch.

Stephanie Farrell & Shell Rose

Down By the Seaside

If they're black send them back,
If they're brown let them drown,
If they're white then they're alright—
'British values' shining bright.
One dead child upon a beach
Now forever out of reach
Of castles built upon the sand,
Of a warm and welcome land.
Lorries steal their last breath
Exchanging dignity for death,
Fortress Europe keeps them out
While politicians scream and shout
Of migrant hordes swarming here—
Feed the hatred, feed the fear
Of losing all that you have got—
So stuff the darkies, fuck the lot.
You need your telly and your 'phone
So why don't you just call home
To where humanity once did dwell
Instead of living in this hell
Where you'd deny a child his life,
A son, a father, mother, wife?
Eton toffs stand coldly by
While people queue up just to die—
Terror, death, their stock in trade...
What lovely sandcastles we all made.

Harry Paterson

This poem has not been forbidden

Yesterday
you walked out of the poem
I wanted to write

I wanted to write
of the space that you left
but your shadow got up
and wrapped itself in night, and followed you
as shadows do*

---

* There was a notice on the wall which said

IT IS FORBIDDEN TO WRITE POEMS
ABOUT THE POOR, THE HUNGRY, OR THE HOMELESS.
ABOVE ALL, IT IS FORBIDDEN
TO WRITE POEMS ABOUT MIGRANTS
WHO MAY HAVE ESCAPED
WAR, HUNGER, TORTURE, FEAR, etcetera,
OR WHO MAY SIMPLY SEEK A BETTER LIFE
(WHICH IS NOT ALLOWED).
IT IS FORBIDDEN TO WRITE POEMS ABOUT MIGRANTS
BECAUSE IT IS NOT FAIR TO USE THEIR LIVES THIS WAY.

Then came, in smaller type

PLEASE UNDERSTAND, THE GOVERNMENT
HAS NOTHING TO DO WITH THIS.
THE GOVERNMENT DEFENDS FREE SPEECH
EXCEPT IN CERTAIN CIRCUMSTANCES OF WHICH, FOR GOOD REASON, IT IS FORBIDDEN TO SPEAK.
THIS IS PURELY IN THE INTEREST
OF THE SUBJECTS OF YOUR POEM
WHO PREFER NOT TO BE EXPLOITED
AND OF YOUR READERS, MOST OF WHOM PREFER
NOT TO BE PREACHED AT, LECTURED OR HECTORED,
AND WHO MOST CERTAINLY PREFER
NEVER TO BE DISTURBED.

Kathleen Bell

Recall

Tony Blair has been recalled to Parliament to answer questions about where his government went wrong with its international policies. He has dyed his hair light brown and grown it all the way to his shoulders. Instead of a tie, he is wearing a collarless shirt. Gone is the haggard look. He is almost his old hippy self. Each time he is asked an awkward question, he shrugs, smiles sheepishly and admits he 'didn't get everything right.' His friend, Alastair, has grown his hair long again, too. He sits nearby, head down like a moody teenager. Every now and again, he exchanges a wink with Tony.

Ian Seed

Quotas

If it is to be four thousand of the most deserving,
four thousand of the most deserving
of the four million currently displaced;
a thousand in a million
of the four million currently camping
in Jordan and in Lebanon—
so, one in a thousand;
one in a thousand
of the four million Syrians—
though not the Afghans or Iraqis
and not the Africans, none of them.
If it's to be these and only them,
these most deserving of the all deserving
filling up the camps—though not the ones
drowning in the sea or suffocating in the trucks;
not the ones crushed on the railroads;
not those babies carried through the night
or held at the stations, dehydrated, close to death.
If just these few—how shall we pick?
Will it be this woman who has lost her home?
Or this man who has lost his legs?
This child orphaned and frightened?
Or this elder, sightless and bent?
If we are to choose
and make of our fences
a new and sturdy pearly gate,
who shall stand watch
at our new beginning?
Who will be Peter

manning a cannon?
Who will record
the ones not taken?
The children washed up
on the beaches
with flotsam.
Who will record them
as undeserving?
Who will save us
when history
remembers?

Lydia Towsey

The Observer Paradox

It takes you a moment to realise
that the man with two boxes of knives
turned away by the wait staff
came to bargain

not stay. You watch him
pause on the threshold, miss
his decision: left or right
as you wonder if this place

is his hundredth today,
or the first, or the fifth. He
pricked the skin of this cafe
so lightly; likely unseen

by the couples, the chattering
families. Will he appear
in the drawing made
by the child over there

with her father? When he gets home,
boxes intact, will the fact that you
saw him make any difference
at all? What's a poem to a person

with a room full of boxes
and boxes of unsold
and unwanted knives?

Tania Hershman

The Year We Don't Talk About

Radio silence. You dial a dreamed-up number
in a phone box, two thousand miles away
at the normal time. Eleni is no longer there,

she lifted your sleeping niece from the cot,
took hold of the little boy's hand and ran,
the keys in her pocket forgot their purpose.

The washing stayed out for thirty years.
Your eldest sister made it back from camp
but wouldn't be big sister anymore.

A receiver fallen from a hook. A siren's tone.
The thud of a parachutist's boot.
The alternative soundtrack for seventy-four.

Maria Taylor

The First Time...

mother decorated the windows of our rooms with
a duck-tape in the shape of the letter X

was the day of my fifth birthday.

The first time, I heard the sound of sirens was a Tuesday,
 and we had just learned the letter W.

Our teacher, a woman with a face round as dough, said:

Let's play a game; now how many words with W can you
 scribble underneath your desks?

The first time a buzzing sound filled our house

I was not awake.

In her nightgown mother carried me to the threshold where
 the pillars were stronger than the cracked walls

and as the windows performed their dance and walls
 crumbled, I dreamt of a world where *war* was just a
 word scribbled underneath wooden desks and wished
 for another first time.

Jasmine Heydari

We Arrive By Truck

She uses the shawl like a flag,
and can't remember how long
they've been waiting at the station,

propped against the battered lilac,
which flowers above open sewers.
She's been told in another part

of the world, people don't even say
grace before a meal. They eat soup
and meat at one sitting.

That's not kohl around her eyes;
it's dark tracks of sleeplessness.
Nights spent beneath the fractured tin roof.

She knows she should give her infant water,
but the orphan children who drank
from the river all disappeared.

The monsoon stained the only photograph
of her son when he was able to smile.
She carried him from the other side of the mountain.

Sally Flint

The Kiss

Name tag pinned to her winter coat,
the kiss still warm on her flushed cheek,
on a hot September morning
she watched her mother walk away.

All day they passed a continuous stream
on the suburban platform,
teachers in armbands,
loud speakers replacing
the hurried murmur
of her mother's voice.

Blinds pulled down,
hot and sweaty in the dim blue lights,
her eyes flickering into the blackness,
shunting from one station to another
deep in a foreign landscape.

They stood in the village hall
surrounded by an eager crowd
waiting for the auction to begin.
Her stomach rumbling
with each child slipping away
into darkness.

Doors opened and closed
until all were housed,
she stood in a stranger's kitchen
and held onto her bag,
surrendering to strange voices and faces.

Rereading those early letters,
a hurried scrawl
with no news of home,
cradling her doll in her arms,
she remembered the warmth
of that last kiss.

She strayed from her mother's memory
abandoned by war and her family.
Her mother's kiss drifting away.

She stands alone
on the site of her old home,
rubble, a few bricks, a saucepan,
an old cushion remained underneath.

She stands alone with no trace
of what she left behind on that day,
when she held her mother's hand.

Emer Davis

The Invader

Her small pretty face framed with black hair
shines like a gem on the shore
her fear glazed eyes are open
her parted lips dead blue.

The clear blue waters of the Mediterranean
wash the little invader.

Nasrin Parvaz

The Humans are Coming

She wants to be an astronaut
crossing black holes and spiralled galaxies to find
extraterrestrial life.

Her big sister pushes the wheelchair
rattling over a chalky path, kicking up pebbles
white as the Milky Way.

And now an Alien kneels in a field
arm extended to furry probe, communing
with the space-buggy girl.

She tells the story of her burnt-out planet
its skeletal, grey rubble, her scattered
iPhone archived family.

Yet Life is an adventure, she believes
that starts in a rubber dinghy, waves rolling
high in a turbulent cosmos.

While her strong-armed sister is Ship's Engineer
this teenager in spectacles, toothy-grinned
sits always at the helm.

Determined to be in the landing-party
she greets every New-World city, every stranger
with a message of peace.

Despite missing her mother, she's bold
as a first-generation Martian who re-configures
the ancient notion of 'home'.

Now the night-sky has Two Sisters, sparks
in a drifting constellation, their camp-fires
pin-pricking our universe.

Siobhan Logan

Based on an interview at the Croatian border

Tracing

The lines are squiggly around Donegal
so my pencil goes slow as I follow the coast
past Dunkineely, St John's Point and on to Killybegs.

Philip O'Riley wanders, peering into inkwells,
half-listening to others bright and beautiful in the hall,
leaving us Catholics alone.

The cliffs of Slieve League are no easier, a tiny tear,
the point squeaks, takes forever to reach past
Belfast and down to the Mountains of Mourne,

then to Dublin and finally Dun Laoghaire.
Philip comes close, leans over: *Teacher's Pet*;
while from the hall I hear all things are wise and wonderful,

which somehow reminds me of Saturday night with uncle Mick
and aunty Mary making a holy show, bawling out the songs
in the Emerald Club, though they wouldn't go back, not now.

Marilyn Ricci

The devil and the deep

Put your daughter on the
dark, dark water, mother.
Her feet are sore from running.

Every path's a danger, mother.

So put her on the cold, the deep, the dark,
dark water.
It's just another path.

Diane Pinnock

survivors pull their weight in apples

Helen Buckingham

The Big House

This is the house we want to live in,
with multiple windows and shutters.
A veranda to absorb sunsets,
gardens that tumble to a golden beach.

This is the house we want to share,
with bright stucco walls;
a doorbell that repeats Clair de la Lune,
flurries of clematis around the front porch.

This is the house we want to have,
its rooms so big we can run across them,
or around pianos, or four-poster beds.
Spacious baths you can step into.

A house with pools and terraces,
for evenings, when friends congregate
to barbecues of free-range steak,
discuss vintage wine stored in cellars.

This endless house, with attics and corners
for spiders to settle, never to feel scared
of being trodden on, or entrapped in jars.
Multi-coloured carpets from floor to wall.

A place where sun finds our faces,
and neighbours share fruit from trees, with smiles.
This is the house we wish for, with no need
for fences. Home to which we all own a key.

Sally Flint

Stories from “The Jungle”

Everything Abdel sees is smeared, despite his glasses.
With the sleeve of a dusty shirt, he pushes grime
from the middle to the edges of his lenses.
They’ve witnessed family fall victim to war crimes.
He could shower for a fortnight and never feel clean.
English is an official language in Sudan.
At sixteen he wants to join relatives already in England.

To dodge military conscription, Sayid, 20, fled from Syria.
Inspired by the story of one of his heroes, William Gibson,
Sayid got to Egypt, then packed on a small boat to Lampedusa,
through Italy to France, from where he can only move on.
On a borrowed laptop he listens to Syrian pop music.
He’d love to cook. He still has to pay a trafficker
weekly for the right to chase lorries to his brother in England.

With a bandaged hand Abdul, 21, tells of imprisonment
and gestures to describe the electric shocks he received
after his arrest by the Sudanese government.
His tribe also harassed by rebel militia. He feels deceived
by traffickers. Despite his razor-wire injury,
he’ll try again. Sudan was an English colony.
He wants to stop looking over his shoulder.

When a tiger stalks, play dead. But it's hard not to run.
When his friends were arrested in Eritrea, Hayat fled
and moved from Ethiopia to Libya and across the
Mediterranean.
He became tiger, his prey an England-bound train. His
hunt failed.
His broken arm cast, he hunkers in a makeshift, tented cave.
A tiger fails nine of ten hunts. He's five down, four more
to brave.
English is the only European language he speaks.

At Baath University in Homs, his English Literature studies
were interrupted by conscription. Firas drew and followed
an isopleth.
Three family members were killed by Syrian government forces,
he couldn't bear to see or be responsible for any more death.
Skin torn by razor-wire, he still dreams of Oxford spires.
Relatives live in several English towns, all with universities.
He wants to use the language he's immersed himself in.

Ziad was a respected lawyer in Daara. Now he fidgets,
grubby and injured from climbing fences, dodging
security and avoiding dogs. The pack of cigarettes
crinkles as he weaves it in his fingers, emptying
a last curl of tobacco. He didn't smoke them but can't finish
with the packet. He translates legal arguments into English.
He wants to join relatives and practise law again.

Emma Lee

These stories are based on newspaper reports. Names have been changed.

Sinking Ship

We finally reach the coast,
and smiles begin to form,
but they boomerang back
as we're turned away again,
again, again, until the ship
cannot take the weight
the hope in our hands,
the rope around our hearts
stretching across waters,
the anchors in our stomachs
waiting for some sweet relief
that will never manifest.

Where do they come from?
Their smiles fall like bananas
from trees, places you go freely
—the borders are closed
here, where we pride ourselves
on free speech. Again, again,
again, we welcome refugees, but
this land is crumbling under
the weight of false promises,
overcrowded prisons and I want
to reach out my hand to stop them
sinking, but, following orders, I can't.

Carmina Masoliver

Safe

Here,
in this place, my place,
a green place, a quiet place,
you will hear children's voices,
happy voices, all at play,
girls dress up, boys play war,
happy war, like film stars.
They are free to roam, mothers
do not fret over them.
Fathers work, granddads watch,
collect them from school, sit
on doorsteps, quietly smoking.
Trees sway in the breeze.
Autumn makes them glow red,
yellow, brown, some stay green.
Blackbirds sing on spring nights.
Cats roll in the dust, dogs
are walked, chickens squawk.
We eat, drink, sleep, make love,
jog, swim, take holidays.
Some of us grow fruit and veg.
No-one tells us what to do,
shouts at us or watches us.
Our houses have stood for years.
Our history is all around.
Our future mostly feels secure.
Here we will stay, or not.
We are free to come and go.
We think we are nothing special,

ordinary human beings,
from here, there, and everywhere.
Just like you. Just like you.
Some of you, from other countries
look at us. Like what you see?

John Ling

Me and War

We are very similar, Norman
Despite the fact you are a virtual character
but I used to see myself in you
I used to read all my pain when you were crying
and the war was exhibiting its ugly boobs like
disfigured whore.
We are very similar my friend
we both put a red novel and a grenade in our khaki bag,
we both can't look at dead cats and we are asked to Fight!!
Have you heard, Norman?
The crash of ribs under that crazy tank!!
It doesn't sound like Emma's voice when singing...
It doesn't sound like the rhythm you used to sing before you
get infected by the dirt of the war or before you see the
dead body of Emma among piles of smashes...
Norman,
Despite the fact you are a virtual character, you shared with
me those horrible nightmares...
We shared seeing together the atrocities in front of us...
hanged bodies of dead women and children...
and all those people walking on their own free will to their
deaths...
cities on fire, burning, and children amused in front of that
terror...
and hunger, hunger, hunger!!
The hunger that forces girls to prostitute and elderly women
to eat the burned dead horses!
It's war, my friend...

It's the worm that devours long years of love, safety, and
beauty in a moment!
Maybe... I was reading my story in you, my unknown friend!!
Maybe we are one person, Norman,
because we both have dreams, songs (of which half are
military)
under our military helmets, and we both wish we were not
born in the time of war!

Ammar Bin Hatim

Song for Guests

'The new arrival of a guest is reason for a feast'
A North African Bedouin Custom

Fear,
and hate
is flung
it weights down
a tar-paulin night as
folk crowd fire warmth
dreaming of dark tunnel
escape with luminous
hands of friendship
held aloft ready to catch...?

Welcome us

We welcome you all
Come... to us

Sleepless knots of men
crouch into bush hides
waiting for smoky vehicles
stowaway with stony
grey lips of newsprint words
pointed to goad or reject?

Welcome us

We welcome you all
Come... to us

Skeins of women children
hold emotions like nets with
wounded screams as
running tears hearts salt
human streams across earth
its seas would it wash away
foul slimes cruel indifference
a dirty din from a baited polis
Is that blood on their hands ?

Welcome us

We welcome you all
Come... be with us
Our table is full
Yet empty missing you

Carol Leeming

Yalla

Shadowed by fissured rock,
fingers funnelling cooling sand,
the pull of the moon carving
the rhythm I need to pierce
the gloom, smell the horizon,
taste futures. I hunker down
to take soft hand to hand as
she quietly asks, who hears?
Who sees? Will land touch us?
Night folds in. Of course, I laugh.
The stars listen, the moon sees,
new land will find us. Yalla!

Yet another dawn,
chin to chest, rib to rib, my
last daughter curves in my lap,
exposed to a firmament fully
intent on pressing our shared
breathe to the depths. I raise
my trailed palm, cool my brow,
wrinkled fingers stroke dreams,
residue all at odds with the tides.
Does anyone tune into the stars?
Who cares what the moon sees?
Will land reach out? Yalla. Yalla!

Trevor Wright

Andy Warhol's Soup Tins

Portraits of hunger are hanging
On the faces of children
In the towns and cities of Donbas
A landscape scrawled on by marauding gunmen

A mother could sketch a bowl of fruit
And wish that still life into existence
If a picture could somehow become real
Let it be Andy Warhol's, the one with the soup tins

Andy Szpuk

Settlers

1

Dropped into a small blue bucket, by little hands
long ago, shells washed up on another shore,
pebbles, hand-picked specimens, sit silent

in a grey morning in the North. Ordinary
seashells perfectly formed, pink and grey stones
washed smooth, veined brown and white,

quartz and jet going nowhere.
How they shine in the cool damp air,
brought here on a one-way ride.

2

Men and women, hauled from their beds,
shunted across weak borders
and set to sweat,

reap another's harvest,
unable to shift, neither East nor West,
halted in the shoes they stood in,

resting now in a new land
of bread and oranges, unable to utter
anything about their half-way house.

Mary Matusz

Poem

The workshop was built wholly and solely for the accommodation of this one inmate and her attendants, some fifty workmen hammering for their lives on sheer copper to complete her tresses
Daily News, *London*

It is autumn 1875
and Parisian workers sculpt a gift
for a sister Republic. Float

copper fingers, toes, eyebrows, nose,
in crates through the Narrows
of New York harbour

land Liberty's limbs
on concrete plinth
laid by Italian immigrants.

Mother of Exiles, tell
a closer, sibling tale;
how Lady Liberty quit Leicester city

just after the Millennium
to perch on a high plinth
above a roundabout.

Those that take the trouble
find the frozen torch of Liberty
doubles as a Mr Whippy

in the arctic breeze
of the Upperton Road
atop five concrete bands

and a plaque of Paine
When men yield up the privilege of thinking,
the last shadow of liberty quits the 'horizon'.

French workmen ascended
through the raised right sole
of Liberty's foot

to extend her reach.
Poor Tom preserve
the swerve of thought

when rights fall alienable;
and he, she, they, we
turn or are turned away.

Simon Perril

Human Being

I type into Google: "What is a human being?"

I look around my humble surroundings; there's a welcoming feel. The caseworkers smile, so does the receptionist. It's a centre for asylum seekers and refugees. Here we are referred to by our names, not numbers. Google swarms with definitions: 'Homo sapiens, distinguished from other animals by superior mental development, power of articulate speech and upright stance'. I glance around: everyone here meets this description. I look for a postscript, 'But once you seek asylum you cease to be human, lose all human rights and hence subject to inhumane treatment.' Phew! Nothing.

Swan

When Hatred Rules

When hatred rules the nations
I choose, without regret,
to be a refugee
among the patriots.

Thomas Orszag-Land

Please look after this bear

In a Budapest park today
the bears woke alone
only a stray sock and sweet wrapper
to remember their carers by.

Dust, sea salt and sand
crust their hobbled paws,
arms droop from walks longer
than their Chinese stitches
had prepared them for.

Their cocoa, pink and honey coats
are grubbily fading from all
they have pillowed and heard,
before ears were left on razor wire
at the Serbian border.

Their soft labels with faint instructions
were twisted through fingers
in lines that stretched to forever
and back again, till there was nothing left
about hand washing at 30 degrees
and never tumble drying polyester.

Nothing printed in all these warnings
about keeping all bears
a safe distance from Sarin gas,
barrel bombs and shrapnel.

Their eyes were sewn and re-sewn
from many a mother's hem
to stop the smaller world collapsing
and now they watch cameras
snatching the park at dawn
whilst the last train heaves.

The bears gaze out
through screens and papers
surrounded by headlines
screaming panic or pity
straining to see
where their children have gone.

Laila Sumpton

Overture

Though the rooms I inhabit are different,
The book-cluttered Canterbury cottage,
The flat on Blackstock Road that judders
With passing buses till the early hours,
Though the rooms I live in are different,

There is always the mole-blind night without
Sleep, no way out of the mishmash of time,
While the low light pitches up preparedly,
Factual as a cleaning lady come to chuck
Away the slops and hardened crusts of yesterday,

Which is the not-ready point of carrying on,
The word *dim* at its most diminished, so sly
That it's then some shy slip of a wing strokes,
Mists in to release fluttery feelings of hope
For brothers and sisters all over the globe.

Alongside workers in Cairo bus queues,
Above beggars supine in Dakar station,
Tracing gazes to the sky from Jenin kitchens,
Scouring the Med's furrowed brow for sight of land:
The end of the line as pivot of inversions,

Untimely fellowships, memories of poems,
Wordsworth's 'Westminster Bridge', Kosztolányi's
'Dawnstruck', august the baton that pauses
To music the silence that we call resonance, call
Because the mortal soundlessness is,

A cemetery of dirt, stone, strewn brown flowers,
Over which umbrellas of rose light rise,
Tendering all the same, the way I love how
That word *surrender* brakes, breaks, caves over
Into yielding, accepting unbroken sea.

Caroline Rooney

My Neighbour

My new neighbour, Ahmad, seems an OK guy.
He volunteers for Age UK, shows me pics
of his wife and kids, talks about the band
he plays in, how he hopes to make
the big time. Then this morning

he tells me he's a refugee. And we all know
they're all illegals. We all know
they come in swarms, surges, floods,
swamp our NHS, take our women, houses, jobs.

So how come Ahmad seems to be
an OK guy, when he's a refugee?

Richard Byrt

Market Day

The man in town who is still angry with the bus driver
who scrutinizes every lemon in the market for bruises
who has heard the ground is good to soft at Kempton
who has a surfeit of betting slips in his coat pocket
who ignores the man playing accordion for coppers
who has travelled across Europe with a Weltmesiter
who watches the rainwater pooling in the gutter
who was taught how to play *sevdalinka* by his brother
the music of longing, which repeats and repeats.

Maria Taylor

No Further

While I stand naked in the bamboo hut
I am my father. Our freckles fuse,
our noses redden, our hair bleaches to sand.

He is marching in the Arakan, his friends
fall at his feet, they die quietly—
Jamchapel (Honeychurch), Windy (Breeze), Oscar (Wild).

At seventy-four my father fights battles in his pyjamas.
He wakes on the floor of his room.
A Lancaster bomber painted on a china plate

climbs the frail wall.
He is marching, the sweat stands on his brow,
his nose glistens. His squadron seeps across

a tea-plantation, one man is invited in to bathe.
My father sits naked in a tin bath.
I ladle water over my shoulders,

come to welcome the knife of water down my back.
The scrubbing brush will not rid my feet of grime,
it lines my toenails like kohl.

Should I wash my hair first or my bucket of clothes?
The tin of water is mine, to dowse my sandals,
to dribble down my legs, to scald away the heat.

Outside, a soldier rests a gun
across his narrow shoulders.
He will patrol the camp tonight.

After nine I will go no further than my hut
with its woven walls and roof of folded leaves.

Chrissie Gittins

Missing

for Shahin Memishi

He is keeping alive
his language, its silky
consonants, its slippery vowels

and the hot colour
of his country's earth
its burned-off skies,

here where it is always
grey and green, grey and green,
the shock of bombs

smothered under neutrals
and people smile
not looking into eyes

for fear of catching fire.
He is afraid too,
but only of forgetting

to yearn. Sometimes
it is good to miss he says,
trying the hard sounds.

A.C. Clarke

Last Rain of the Season

Each empty chair greeted
with that sort of touch
kept for a childhood pony

Paint brushes propped
in an old honey pot to flower again

The key is heavy
Heavy and cold
She turns thoughts
to the light pounding at the window
for admission or forgiveness
and with a prayer
steadies to another day

A snail on the doorstep
She moves it gently so very gently away

Kevin Jackson

People like to make films about me

They like to tell my story.
I would like to tell my own story.
I would like to tell my story in my own way.
I do not know what you mean by 'subaltern'.
I have never wanted a rank.
I'm not below others who have a human face.
I am not above the whales or the tigers.
I do not know what you mean by 'bare life'.
My life is dear to me.
It is dear to me whether I live it in a leaky tent or in a
    maisonette
Or in some waiting room.
Why don't you ask me about that day, that day
I laid face down in a field of marigolds high above the
    coastal planes,
Or that night, when the stars were thick and close, before
    the soldiering began...
Or why not just ask me about the sweetened black tea and
    goat's cheese?
Or ask me about the moped I left behind.
I thank you for your offer to write a poem about me.
I hope you'll excuse the little I've sent on.
As for me? I'd like to direct a movie, to bring you
The bringing of where I am from.
You'll see. It won't be the same as the words about me.

Caroline Rooney

Ironing Out

after an appeal for unwanted men's clothes

Deposited, a heap
of slightly soiled goodwill
towards the desperate
from Sri Lanka, Syria,
Iran, Somalia, the men
detained. Can clothes
remember? Can they be
reminded how their former
wearers wore them, changed
out of them, changed
as they chose? Long past
choosing, these ones slumped
in plastic bags. I'll
try it though, try ironing
a once expensive shirt
so flat each sleeve becomes
a blue-print for an arm
to swing at ease and to
and fro at liberty. And
as for someone's rumpled
quite good trousers I'll
press the legs so crisply,
creases sharp as blades,
they stand, in highly polished
shoes perhaps, and take
such briskly clattering steps
detaining bars or barriers
rise to let them through
and no word said but Sir.

Hubert Moore

In truth I was afraid

Keleti station, Hungary
2 September 2015

At Keleti station we are confronted by stacks of men
decked in black, dark glasses, heads shaved, arms crossed,
hands readied on weapons, and the enemy is where?

Is it we who have disembarked, holding tickets?
It is not. But we are nervous as police—militarised,
dystopian—corral us, block normal routes.

Still we cannot locate the enemy till we peer down
a sweep of steps and at their base a grille
and behind it in ashy light penned-in people.

Seeing appears forbidden and in the atmosphere
—you could cut it with a knife—of tamped-down
violence we follow orders, step away and exit.

Outside multitudes of huddled people, arraigned
on concrete, their youth demonstrating.
Next we descend to the underground harbouring

the shut-away people, take small steps around them.
The smell is of sweat and fear and no sign of a toilet.
And yet the children play.

Joan Byrne

Framed

Mum always covered her head
before leaving the house;
and, of course, in our place of worship.

Cotton, sometimes chiffon or printed:
A Present from Skegness, framed high
cheek bones, flattened bouncy curls.

Her mum wore a hat, even at tea,
her grandmother, a long woollen shawl
gathered with a pin beneath her chin.

Today, a daughter-in-law in the village shop,
hijab framing big brown eyes.

Marilyn Ricci

Home/Homesickness/Homeless

The Russian across the street is whistling
and you wonder
how many languages they will make you chase
before the ground beneath the stones
stops moving.

There is a word for it, perhaps, in some language
but you cannot invent it.
And so you move around the room imitating
the random goldenness that permeates

the edges of leaves, the tops of gates,
the periphery of shadows,
pulling everything into its void of static melancholy
and yet, you're not sad.

This stillness is the erasure of stupefaction
like being poured unconsciously into rounded glass.
You feel it penetrate through the window
speaking through the warmth of the sun

that gradually cools behind the house,
with a curdled silence that draws a curtain around the room,
temporarily warming your skin,
but leaving you strangely aching when the heat disappears.

Hila Shachar

Killing

Watching his son playing
memories flooded his mind
of the time, when unemployed and desperate
he had joined the Black Water Army.

He clasped his son,
as the eyes of the young men he had tortured and killed
flashed across his mind, threatening vengeance.

Nasrin Parvaz

Hayride

"I feel like a refugee," my friend says
as we lean on the trailer side behind
the sliding tractor.

I say nothing, but imagine a paralysis
brought on by shock, the shadow of fear
falling across these scattered bales

as our children sit, jittery and wired
to the scroll of scouring jets, while behind us,
everything burns.

Roy Marshall

From A North Atlantic Island

~~*A broken sonnet, after Barry Cole*~~

No ... is an island, but this ..
~~You have come to the wrong place~~
Do not wait for the tide to ....
~~Our people are better off without you~~
We do not .... that this ...... is of ... ... making
~~Find a place that cares more~~
We ..... to work towards an .... solution
~~Don't try to embarrass us, for we will not relent~~
There is .... and there are ..... for you to .... in
~~If our feckless poor donate their food, that's up to them~~
Understand that we are a caring ....
~~Just don't confuse compassion with concern~~
You will .... for yourselves when it's time to go
~~If we stop bombing your home, we'll let you know~~

David Belbin

Children of War

Every child in my land suffers torment of wars.

Every child in my land suckles milk mixed with fear.

I ache, ache from the gun at my side:
your gift, Father, the day before they killed you.

You told me your gun would be my best friend.
It has been with me each day and each night. And still

Every child in my land suffers torrents of wars.

Every child in my land suckles milk mixed with fear.

Malka Al-Haddad

Dislocation

Days pass

become
one long day
words run away—

mountain   sanity   salt

shadows
sound like trains

Nights on trains

become
one long night
words fly—

passport   pushchair   rights

Waiting at borders
like birds
on precarious perches where

shadows
sound like rain

smell like pain

Pam Thompson

Through the Lens

a bus stops
the crowd surges forward
a frantic rush and crush

Zoom in...
  small arms clinging
    around a man's neck
  a frail old lady
    hoisted aboard
  a clinging hand-hold
    broken

Long shot...
  bus disappearing
  makeshift camp re-settling
  light and hope fading

Zoom out...
  empty water bottles
  arranged in a circle
  and three blankets
  two small and one long
  bent into a gentle curve
  making a perfect smiley face

Liz Byfield

Breathing from a Permanent Home

Rattling like dice
mottled in terror
more and more arrive each day

Clutching their hands
on their hearts
pushed through your screen

sneaked in on boats
the report said
dancing across the flames

hogtied in divisions
scooped up and down
the panorama

pleading we must
care about their plight
clouded in ghostly shapes

floating in a cul-de-sac
of broken projections

instead of just breathing

breathing.

breathing.

Andy N

but one country

our home
is but one country
truly, the whole earth
is there for them to settle
tell us if you can, where else
shall we go when they have come?
they do not belong in our homeland
you should blush when you say to us
we must turn our vision up-side down

we must turn our vision up-side down
you should blush when you say to us
they do not belong in our homeland
shall we go when they have come?
tell us if you can, where else
is there for them to settle
truly, the whole earth
is but one country
our home

Rod Duncan

and the sea did give up those dead in it

Revelation 20:13

privilege enjoy those as me suffer I around great immeasurably
I as great me privilege enjoy around immeasurably suffer those
privilege me those as around I great enjoy suffer immeasurably
around great as suffer privilege I enjoy those immeasurably me
me immeasurably those as suffer great enjoy I around privilege
those suffer me enjoy around immeasurably great I privilege as
around me great suffer immeasurably I enjoy those privilege as
enjoy privilege suffer those around me immeasurably great I as
me as great privilege those immeasurably I around suffer enjoy
as those around me enjoy great suffer I privilege immeasurably
as I suffer great privilege those around me enjoy immeasurably
as I enjoy immeasurably those around me suffer great privilege
as I suffer immeasurably those around me enjoy great privilege
as I enjoy great privilege those around me suffer immeasurably

Daniel O'Donnell-Smith

At the Border

A bird flitters
through air, unhindered
by the razor wire.

A man flees,
but he is trapped
by the fence.

A night-moth plays
in the headlights,
then leaves.

A child clings—
she trusts,
she believes.

A worm pushes
through earth,
dissolving.

Alison Lock

Contributors

Malka Al-Haddad is an Iraqi academic who has lived in Britain since 2012. She is a member of the Union of Iraqi Writers, Director of the Women's Center for Arts and Culture in Iraq, and an activist with Leicester City of Sanctuary.

Alan Baker grew up in Newcastle-upon-Tyne and has lived in Nottingham since 1985, where he runs poetry publisher Leafe Press. His most recent poetry collections are *all this air and matter* (Oystercatcher) and *Whether* (KFS).

David Belbin is best known for his novels and short stories, but has been publishing poems (one or two a decade) since 1975. His latest novel is *The Great Deception* (Freight Books).

James Bell was born in Scotland and lives in Brittany where he contributes non-fiction and photography to an English language journal. He has published two collections of poetry: *the just vanished place* (2008) and *fishing for beginners* (2010).

Kathleen Bell's pamphlet *at the memory exchange* (Oystercatcher, 2014) was shortlisted for the Saboteur awards. She lives in Nottingham and teaches Creative Writing at De Montfort University.

Ammar Bin Hatim was born in Kirkuk, Iraq, in 1978. His first collection of poems, *Ramad Al-Teen*, was published in Cairo in 2013. He is also an artist.

Helen Buckingham's collections include *water on the moon* and *mirrormoon* (Original Plus Press, 2010) and *Armadillo Basket* (Waterloo Press, 2011). She is fortunate to have been born with a roof over her head in London and to continue to live likewise in Wells, Somerset.

Liz Byfield lives in Leicestershire. She began writing poetry recently following a lifetime in education. She enjoys open mic sessions and recently performed at the Radnor Fringe Festival.

Joan Byrne has been published in *Obsessed with Pipework*, *South Bank Poetry*, and webzine *Ink, Sweat & Tears*. A nominee for the 2014 Pushcart Prize, she is one of three Rye Poets who regularly perform in London. www.joanbyrne.co.uk

Richard Byrt has recently published his first pamphlet, *Devil's Bit* (De Montfort Books, 2015). He volunteers with an LGBT oral history project and helps people with mental health problems to tell their stories.

Russell Christie, a Nottingham-based novelist, is a long-time LGBT civil rights activist and speaker. His most recent novel is *The Queer Diary of Mordred Vienna.*

A.C. Clarke's fourth collection, *In The Margin*, is published by Cinnamon Press. Her pamphlet *A Natural Curiosity* was shortlisted for the 2012 Callum Macdonald Memorial Award and she has been longlisted for the National Poetry Competition. She lives in Glasgow.

Merrill Clarke took up writing poetry for his own amusement when he retired from his work as a university lecturer. He attends poetry workshops and open mic events around Leicester.

Emer Davis has recently returned home to Ireland from Abu Dhabi. She has performed her work in both countries and has published the print book of poems *Kill Your Television* as well as two ebooks.

Anne de Gruchy was born in London but has felt at home in the East Midlands since arriving more than thirty years ago. She is a writer, mental health advocate and carer for her father. Her blog is www.annedegruchy.co.uk

Richard Devereux is a member of the Lansdown Poets in Bristol. He has recently contributed poems to the website *The Stare's Nest.*

Welsh-born **Rod Duncan** lives in Leicester where he teaches creative writing at De Montfort University. His novel *The Bullet Catcher's Daughter* was shortlisted for the Philip K. Dick Award and the East Midlands Book Award.

Ken Evans is a prize-winning poet who lives in the Peak District.

Stephanie Farrell is primarily a prose writer, but dabbles in poetry and pop culture articles. After studying Creative Writing and English at De Montfort University, she moved to London and is currently completing her first novel.

Kerry Featherstone is Creative Writing Lecturer at Loughborough University. His poems have been widely published and he is also a songwriter.

Sally Flint is a lecturer in Creative Writing/English Literature at the University of Exeter. She co-founded and edits *Riptide Journal* and *Canto Poetry*, and also works with 'Stories Connect'. Her recent collections are *Pieces of Us* (Worple Press) and the chapbook *The Hospital Punch* (Maquette Publications).

Neil Fulwood is a published poet and fiction writer, author of *The Films of Sam Peckinpah* and co-editor, with David Sillitoe, of *More Raw Material: work inspired by Alan Sillitoe.*

Chrissie Gittins' poetry collections are *Armature* (Arc) and *I'll Dress One Night As You* (Salt). Her third pamphlet collection is *Professor Heger's Daughter* (Paekakariki Press). She also publishes short fiction and children's poetry. www.chrissiegittins.co.uk

Mark Goodwin is a widely-published poet-sound-artist and community poet, who encourages all kinds of people to experience through poetry and poetics. Born in Oxford in 1969, he was brought up on a farm in Leicestershire. Mark has two growing-up children.

Jan Harris was born in Nottinghamshire. Her poems have recently appeared in *Snakeskin*, *Envoi*, *Abridged* and *Poems for a Liminal Age*. Her tanka was displayed at *The Colour of Poetry* exhibition.

Tania Hershman is the author of two short story collections from Tangent Books and Salt and co-author of *Writing Short Stories: A Writers' & Artists' Companion* (Bloomsbury, 2014). Her debut poetry chapbook is forthcoming in February 2016. She curates ShortStops (www.shortstops.info), is a Royal Literary Fund fellow at Bristol University and is studying for a PhD in Creative Writing at Bath Spa University. www.taniahershman.com

Jasmine Heydari is Iranian by descent but brought up in Sweden. Her poems are inspired by her own experiences of the Iran-Iraq war and the years which followed. She is a freelance writer and translator currently working on her first novel.

Anne Holloway is Professional Development Manager for Mouthy Poets and has just published her first novel. She is a graduate of Nottingham Trent University where she gained an MA in Creative Writing. A member of Nottingham Writers Studio, she believes it is never too late to start writing.

Danielle Hope is a doctor and poet living in London. She founded and edited *Zenos*, worked for Survivors' Poetry, and is advisory editor for *Acumen* literary magazine. Her 2015 collection, *Mrs Uomo's Yearbook*, is published by Rockingham Press. www.daniellehope.org

Louisa Humphreys lives in Leicester where she works as a museum assistant.

Sally Jack is a writer, editor and poet based in Leicester. She co-created and co-runs Upstairs at the Western, Leicester's first pub theatre and is Media Manager of Off the Fence Theatre Company. Sally regularly reviews for *British Theatre Guide* and is Spoken Word (Midlands) editor with *Sabotage Reviews*.

Kevin Jackson has published online, in journals and anthologies, in the US and Europe. He views poetry writing as activism and is fascinated by its capacity to engender community empowerment. Kevin moved to the East Midlands in 2013 and has recently discovered the pleasures of a campervan. He blogs at kevnjacksn.wordpress.com

Martin Johns lives in Northamptonshire.

Penny Jones is a writer from Leicester with a special interest in flash fiction. She came second in the University of Leicester's short story competition and her first short story will be published in 2016 by Fox Spirit Books. She attends the monthly meet up of Leicester Writes and was involved in the first Leicester Writes festival for new writers.

Ziba Karbassi was born in Tabriz, Iran. She left her country with her mother in the late 1980s and has mostly since lived in London. She has published ten books of poetry in Persian, and two in English and Italian. She was chairperson of the Iranian Writers Association (in exile) from 2002-2004, editor of *Asar* and an editor for *Exiled Ink*. She was chair of Exiled Writers Ink in UK year 2012-2014.

Emma Lee has published three poetry collections: *Ghosts in the Desert* (Indigo Dreams, 2015), *Mimicking a Snowdrop* (Thynks, 2014) and *Yellow Torchlight and the Blues* (Original Plus 2004). She reviews for *The Journal, Sabotage Reviews* and *London Grip*, and blogs at emmalee1.wordpress.com

Carol Leeming was born in Leicester and raised in both Leicester and Jamaica. Published in a number of anthologies, Carol is a successful multi-disciplinary artist, working in music, literature and digital media. Her choreopoem *The Loneliness of the Long Distance Diva* (Curve Theatre) was part of the 2012 Cultural Olympiad. Carol is a Fellow of the Royal Society of the Arts.

Joanne Limburg has published two collections with Bloodaxe Books, as well as a memoir, a book of poems for children, and a pamphlet, *The Oxygen Man* (Five Leaves, 2012). Her most recent book is the novel, *A Want of Kindness*. She lives in Cambridge with her husband and son.

John Ling has been a children's librarian, a teacher of the deaf and in the Kirklees Autism Outreach Service. He is a Quaker and community mediator. His books include *Social Stories for Kids in Conflict* (Speechmark) and the poetry collection *Alice the Healer* (Authorhouse). He divides his time between mediation and conflict resolution, working for the Alternatives to Violence Project.

Alison Lock's poetry and short stories have appeared in many anthologies and journals. She is the author of a short story collection, two poetry collections, and a forthcoming fantasy novella. She has an MA in Literature Studies. She is a tutor for courses of Transformative Life Writing.

Siobhan Logan's *Firebridge to Skyshore: A Northern Lights Journey* and *Mad, Hopeless and Possible: Shackleton's Endurance Expedition* (both Original Plus Press) have been performed at the British Science Museum and Leicester's National Space Centre. In 2014 she led WEM's first-ever digital writing residency. Her latest obsession is space. siobhanlogan.blogspot.co.uk

Aoife Mannix is the author of four collections of poetry and a novel. She has been poet in residence for the Royal Shakespeare Company and BBC Radio 4's *Saturday Live*. She has performed throughout the UK and toured internationally with the British Council. She has a PhD in creative writing from Goldsmiths, University of London. She currently blogs at livingasanalien.wordpress.com

Roy Marshall lives in Leicestershire. His work in adult education has afforded him the pleasure of meeting people for whom English is not a first language, many of whom are working hard to make a new life in the UK. Roy's poetry collection, *The Sun Bathers* (2013) is published by Shoestring Press.

Carmina Masoliver is a writer, poet and performer and part of the *Burn After Reading* community, and *Kid Glove* collective. She has been published as part of *Nasty Little Press' Intro* series, has performed at festivals and facilitates workshops. She edits the anthology *Poetry&Paint* and runs the *She Grrrowls* event in London.

Mary Matusz lives in Huddersfield where there is a thriving poetry community. Her parents were Polish refugees who settled in Britain after the Second World War. They were not able to return but Mary has visited Poland many times.

John Mingay lives in Scotland, is a widely published poet and was editor of Raunchland Publications.

Alan Mitchell writes "I was once a junkie./ I am no longer a junkie./ I am a drop out./I have always been a drop out./ I renounce this misanthropic, mono-cultural, militaristic, materialist mindset that passes itself off as normalcy for the masses./ I have an ambition./ It is called *Peace & Plenty for All.*"

Hubert Moore has published eight collections of poems, the last four with Shoestring. One of his poems, 'Hosing Down', was included in the 2015 Forward anthology. He is a long-term supporter of and writer about refugees, having been a Detainee visitor and, at 'Freedom from Torture', a writing mentor.

Ambrose Musiyiwa facilitates CivicLeicester, a community media channel that uses video and photography to document and highlight conversations taking place in and around Leicester. He is the author of *The Gospel According to Bobba*, a slim volume of poems that range in subjects from challenges and fears to the joys of a cup of tea and biscuits.

Andy N is a poet, writer and musician from Manchester. His most recent book is *and the end of summer*. His website is onewriterandhispc.blogspot.co.uk

Daniel O'Donnell-Smith is a PhD student in Creative Writing at Birkbeck College. His chapbook <c>*Odes* is published by Leafe Press.

Thomas Orszag-Lund (b. 1938) is a poet and award-winning journalist. He survived the Holocaust, participated in the 1956 Budapest revolution against Soviet rule as a cub reporter on *The Hungarian Independent*, read philosophy in Acadia University, Canada, and served as a correspondent for the London *Observer* and *The New York Times*. His last book was *Survivors: Hungarian Jewish Poets of the Holocaust* (Smokestack, 2014).

Nasrin Parvaz was born in Tehran. In post-revolutionary Iran she became a women's and civil rights activist. She was arrested, tortured and imprisoned for eight years. She fled to England, where she claimed asylum in 1993. She studied for a degree in Psychology, gained an MA in International Relations, then trained as a therapist. Nasrin's prison memoir was published in Farsi in 2002. Working with poet Hubert Moore, Nasrin has translated poems prohibited in Iran from Farsi into English. They appear in the *Modern Poetry in Translation* series.

Harry Paterson is a freelance music journalist. He has also written *Look Back in Anger: the Miners' Strike in Nottinghamshire* and *Making Plans for Nigel: a beginner's guide to Farage and UKIP* (both Five Leaves).

Simon Perril's most recent poetry publications are *Beneath: a Nekyiad* and *Archilochus on the Moon* (Shearsman 2015 and 2013). As a critic he has written widely on contemporary poetry, editing books on John James and Brian Catling. He is Reader in Contemporary Poetic Practice at De Montfort University, Leicester.

Mariya Pervez is a student.

A latecomer to authorship, **Diane Pinnock** now writes poems and short stories and reads her work at spoken word events, or to anyone who will listen. For almost 30 years, she's had a day job in criminal justice, and lives in Nottingham with her husband, two daughters, and cat, Bruce, who likes to walk over her keyboard when she writes.

Sheenagh Pugh is half Welsh, half Irish and lives in Shetland. She has published many collections of poetry with Seren, of which the latest is *Short Days, Long Shadows* (Seren 2014). She has also published two novels and a critical study of fan fiction.

Mark Rawlins is a grumpy old git who writes and performs poetry as an outlet for his anger and frustration. He has performed at poetry slams, open mic nights, and anywhere else where they'll have him all over the North West of England. He is a leading figure in Macclesfield's blossoming poetry and spoken word scene.

Marilyn Ricci lives in Leicestershire. Her work has appeared in anthologies and many magazines including *Magma*, *The Rialto* and *Modern Poetry In Translation*. Her pamphlet *Rebuilding a Number 39* is published by Happenstance Press.

Caroline Rooney is an arts activist and Professor of African and Middle Eastern Studies at the University of Kent. Her poetry appears in *In Protest: 150 Poems for Human Rights*. She has directed and produced documentary films and mounted performance events on refugee experiences.

Shell Rose is a freelance writer and is interested in all aspects of creative writing, from the tame to the experimental. She has a BA in Creative Writing and English from De Montfort University, lives in Leicester and writes a weekly blog, Fibro Forever.

Sibyl Ruth, a Birmingham-based poet, has translated the poems her German-Jewish great-aunt Rose Scooler wrote in the Theresienstadt Ghetto.

Chrys Salt's work has been performed internationally and been translated into several languages. *The Burning* was selected as one of the 20 Best Scottish Poems 2012. In 2014 her pamphlet *Weaver of Grass* was shortlisted for the Callum Macdonald Memorial Award and she was awarded a Writers Bursary and an MBE for Services to the Arts.

Barbara Saunders's life has been defined by immigration. The grandchild of Russian immigrants, she stayed in an absorption centre abroad, meeting other immigrants from all over the world. She now teaches English to the children of immigrants from China, India, Pakistan, Ethiopia, Iraq, Iran, Serbia.

Rose Scooler (1881–1985) composed and memorised her poems in the Theresienstadt Ghetto. After Theresienstadt was liberated at the end of the war she was taken to a Displaced Persons Camp at Deggendorf in Bavaria. Eventually she emigrated to the United States. Her poems were found after her son's death in 2006.

Ian Seed's collections of poetry include *Makers of Empty Dreams* (2014), *Shifting Registers* (2011) and *Anonymous Intruder* (2009), all from Shearsman. His work is represented in Salt's *Best British Poetry 2014*. He teaches at the University of Chester.

Hila Shachar is a Lecturer in English Literature at De Montfort University and a writer for The Australian Ballet. Her book, *Cultural Afterlives and Screen Adaptations of Classic Literature: Wuthering Heights and Company* (Palgrave Macmillan, 2012), was nominated for the 2012 Western Australian Premier's Book Awards. She has published fiction, critical work and essays.

Lily Silverman is a graduate and child of a Jewish refugee father who survived Buchenwald. In 1935 when Lily's father was 15 his German citizenship was withdrawn by the Nazis. Lily's son had his German citizenship was restored in 2015 when he was 15. Lily and her son speak at schools in the UK and Germany about life growing up in a refugee family.

Mahendra Solanki was born in Nairobi of Indian parents and his work draws upon this background. Since the publication of *Shadows of My Making* in 1986, his poems have appeared in magazines and anthologies in Britain and abroad and broadcast by the BBC. He is a Royal Literary Fund Fellow at the University of Warwick and a practising psychotherapist.

Laila Sumpton divides her time between working at international children's charity Plan UK and as a freelance poet. She regularly performs her poetry on human rights themes and co-edited the Human Rights Consortium's anthology *In Protest: 150 poems for human rights* (2012). She is a member of the Keats House Poets and is working on her first collection.

Swan is the pen-name of a fifty year old Zimbabwean woman and asylum seeker (still waiting for asylum to be granted) who has lived in the UK for almost 16 years. Since she was a child she has written stories which have ended up in her scrap box. The creative writing skills group in Nottingham has helped her gain confidence; she now writes more, and is an avid reader.

George Symonds is a law student. As a British citizen in the UK, he fell foul of the financial criteria required for his wife's spouse visa, as she is a non-EU/EEA national. Because he earns less than £18,600 per year, the Conservative government deemed family life a 'privilege' he doesn't deserve. He finds poetry cathartic and blogs at www.guiltynation.wordpress.com

Andy Szpuk is a novelist, short story writer, memoirist and poet based in Nottingham. His debut, *Sliding on the Snow Stone*, is the true story of one Ukrainian man's journey through famine, Soviet terrors, and Nazi occupation in World War Two. Andy is a member of DIY Poets performance poetry collective in Nottingham.

Laura Taylor has been writing and performing poetry since 2010, and will continue to do so whilst injustices are wreaked against the poor and vulnerable. You may find more of her work at www.writeoutloud.net/profiles/laurataylor

Maria Taylor's poems have been published in a range of magazines including *Ambit*, *Magma* and *The Rialto*. Her first collection *Melanchrini* (Nine Arches Press) was shortlisted for the Michael Murphy Memorial Prize. Her mother's family was exiled from Northern Cyprus in 1974.

Pam Thompson is a poet and university lecturer. Her publications include collections *The Japan Quiz* (Redbeck Press, 2008) and *Show Date and Time* (Smith-Doorstop, 2006). She was a recent winner of the Judge's Prize in the *Magma* Poetry Competition. Pam co-organises Word!, a spoken word open mic night at The Y Theatre in Leicester.

Lydia Towsey is a poet and performer. Her commissions include: *Freedom Showcase*; *Spoken Word All Stars Tour* and *Beyond Words*. She has spoken at the House of Lords, performed at London's 100 Club and presented at Plymouth University's Zombie Symposium. Her full length collection, *The Venus Papers*, is published by Burning Eye Books. www.secretagentartist.wordpress.com

Rory Waterman's debut collection *Tonight the Summer's Over* (Carcanet, 2013) was a PBS Recommendation. He writes for the *TLS*, co-edits *New Walk* and is lecturer in English at Nottingham Trent University. www.rorywaterman.com

Stephen Watts's translations of Ziba Karbassi's work have appeared in journals including *Poetry Review* and *Modern Poetry in Translation*.

Gregory Woods is emeritus professor of gay and lesbian studies at Nottingham Trent University. His most recent full poetry collections from Carcanet are *Quidnunc* (2007) and *An Ordinary Dog* (2011). His new critical book *Homintern: How Gay Culture Liberated the Modern World* will be published by Yale University Press in 2016. www.gregorywoods.co.uk

Trevor Wright works in adult social care and began writing in his fifties. He is a member of Derby City Poets and Hello Hubmarine and recently contributed to Derby Museum's *Taxidermy Tales*. A member of the Nottingham Writers Studio and the DIY Poetry Collective, he participates in local open mic sessions and facilitates writing for wellbeing workshops.

Peter Wyton is a prize-winning page and performance poet. He lives in Gloucester.

Acknowledgments

This anthology was prompted by a suggestion from Ambrose Musiyiwa and has come into being thanks to the work of very many people. All the poets, editors and publishing staff have given their work and/or time free of charge.

Some of the poems have been published previously as follows.

'The Election Candidates Promise to be Tough on the Causes of Disorder' by Alan Baker in *Variations on Painting a Room: Poems 2000-2010* (Skysill Press)

Haiku (p38) by Helen Buckingham in *Sonic Boom #2*

Haiku (p83) by Helen Buckingham in *Sonic Boom #3*

'Missing' by A.C. Clarke in *Breathing Each Other In* (Blinking Eye Press)

'The Kiss' by Emer Davis, *CTIN 95* (Poetry Kit 2010), *To Tear Your Breath Away*

'We Arrive by Truck' and 'The Big House' by Sally Flint in *Pieces of Us* (Worple Press)

'Frontiers' by Chrissie Gittins in *Professor Heger's Daughter* (Paekakariki Press)

'No Further' by Chrissie Gittins in *Armature* (Arc)

'The Observer Paradox' by Tania Hershman by the Charles Causley Trust, having been commended in the 2014 Charles Causley Poetry Competition

'Relativity' by Tania Hershman in *New Boots and Pantisocracies*

'The First Time' by Jasmine Heydari, won the War Poetry for Today competition run by TheatreCloud in 2014

‘Exodus’ by Danielle Hope in *Mrs Uomo’s Yearbook* (Rockingham)

‘Snow fall’ by Danielle Hope in *Giraffe Under a Grey Sky* (Rockingham) and *Fire*

‘Backscatter Song’ and ‘So Many Set Out’ by Joanne Limburg in *Paraphernalia* (Bloodaxe)

‘Relative’ by Roy Marshall in *Clear Poetry*

‘Hayride’ by Roy Marshall in *The Rialto*

‘The Man who Ran Through The Tunnel’ by Ambrose Musiyiwa in *International Policy Digest* and *The Stare’s Nest*

‘journeying’ by Ambrose Musiyiwa in *Three the Hard Way #whoisyourneighbour*

‘Framed’ by Marilyn Ricci in *Penniless Press*

‘Tracing’ by Marilyn Ricci in *Magma*

‘The Insurrection of Poetry’ by Chrys Salt in *Dancing on a Rock* (Indigo Dreams Publishing)

‘A Memorable Journey’ by Barbara Saunders on Carol Rumens’ blog at *The Guardian – Poem of the Week* (25/8/15)

‘*from* The Riverside Commission’ by Mahendra Solanki in *The Lies We Tell* (Shoestring)

‘Landing on Lampedusa’ by Laila Sumption in *indiefeeds* (audio recording)

‘Andy Warhol’s Soup Tins’ by Andy Szpuk in *DIY Poets* (Nottingham)

‘The Year We Don’t Talk About’ and ‘Market Day’ by Maria Taylor in *Melanchrini* (Nine Arches Press)

‘Ave Maria’ by Rory Waterman in *PN Review*

‘Life History’ by Gregory Woods in *The District Commissioner’s Dreams* (Carcanet)

Financial Support

51 people pledged financial support for this project through our crowdfunder, enabling all the proceeds of the book to go to support refugees, with additional funding from Ross Bradshaw, Jane Brennan, Roger Bromley, Merrill Clarke, Beth Hartshorne, Emma Lee, Siobhan Logan and Bali Rai.

In addition, Everyone's Reading Festival (Leicester) generously gave a community grant, and the spoken word poetry group Mouths Wide Shut (London) organised a fundraising evening for the anthology.